Author:

Tom Ratliff has a master's degree in early American history and teaches history and secondary education at Central Connecticut State University. He is a co-author of the Matty Trescott series—young adult historical novels set in the Civil War era—and writes for the national Newspapers in Education program. His link is www.mattytrescott.com.

Artist:

Mark Bergin was born in Hastings, England, in 1961. He studied at Eastbourne College of Art and specializes in historical reconstructions, aviation, and maritime subjects. He lives in Bexhill-on-Sea with his wife and children.

Series creator:

David Salariya was born in Dundee, Scotland. He has illustrated a wide range of books and has created and designed many new series for publishers in the UK and overseas. David established The Salariya Book Company in 1989. He lives in Brighton, England, with his wife, illustrator Shirley Willis, and their son Jonathan.

Editor: **Stephen Haynes**

Editorial Assistants: **Mark Williams, Jamie Pitman**

© The Salariya Book Company Ltd MMIX
No part of this publication may be reproduced in whole or in part, or stored in a retrieval system, or transmitted in any form or by any means, electronic, mechanical, photocopying, recording, or otherwise, without written permission of the publisher. For information regarding permission, write to the copyright holder.

Published in Great Britain in 2009 by
The Salariya Book Company Ltd
25 Marlborough Place, Brighton BN1 1UB

ISBN-13: 978-0-531-21328-5 (lib. bdg.)   978-0-531-20519-8 (pbk.)
ISBN-10: 0-531-21328-5 (lib. bdg.)   0-531-20519-3 (pbk.)
All rights reserved.
Published in 2010 in the United States
by Franklin Watts
An imprint of Scholastic Inc.
Published simultaneously in Canada.

A CIP catalog record for this book is available
from the Library of Congress.

Printed and bound in China.
Printed on paper from sustainable sources.

SCHOLASTIC, FRANKLIN WATTS, and associated logos are trademarks and/or registered trademarks of Scholastic Inc.

PAPER FROM SUSTAINABLE FORESTS

You Wouldn't Want to Work on the Brooklyn Bridge!

An Enormous Project that Seemed Impossible

Written by
Tom Ratliff

Illustrated by
Mark Bergin

Created and designed by
David Salariya

Franklin Watts®
An Imprint of Scholastic Inc.
NEW YORK • TORONTO • LONDON • AUCKLAND • SYDNEY
MEXICO CITY • NEW DELHI • HONG KONG
DANBURY, CONNECTICUT

Contents

Introduction

You are Washington Roebling, son of the famous engineer John Augustus Roebling. You live in Trenton, New Jersey, with your wife, Emily.

Your father owns a factory that makes cables out of wire rope. He has also designed and built suspension bridges that use his cables. In 1867, he received approval to build a 1,595-foot (486-m)* suspension bridge across the East River, connecting the cities of Brooklyn and New York. You're expecting to be your father's assistant on this thrilling project.

But, tragically, your father will not live to build the bridge he envisioned. Just before construction is due to begin, he dies after a freak accident. The task of building the great bridge now falls to you. Are you ready for the challenge?

*That's just the main span.

It's going to be the longest bridge in the world!**

**until 1903

Emily Warren Roebling
1843–1903

John Augustus Roebling
1806–1869

Washington A. Roebling
1837–1926

John Augustus Roebling

Your father, John Augustus Roebling, was born in 1806 in what is now Germany. He studied engineering and architecture before moving to the United States in 1831. He worked on several canals in Pennsylvania, where ropes were used to haul boats over the mountains on railroad tracks. Ordinary rope is made of interwoven strands of fiber—usually cotton or hemp—and can wear out. John Roebling witnessed a serious accident when a 9-inch (230-mm) hemp rope snapped under the heavy weight of a canal boat. Roebling developed a method of making rope out of iron wire. His new rope was much stronger than hemp and would not wear out with use.

In 1844, Roebling began designing suspension bridges that used his new wire rope. He built bridges over the Delaware, Ohio, and Niagara rivers, and in 1855 proposed a bridge over New York's East River.

JOHN ROEBLING'S Niagara River Bridge, which opened in 1855, could carry both rail and road traffic. Its main span was 821 feet (250 m) long. The bridge remained in use until 1897.

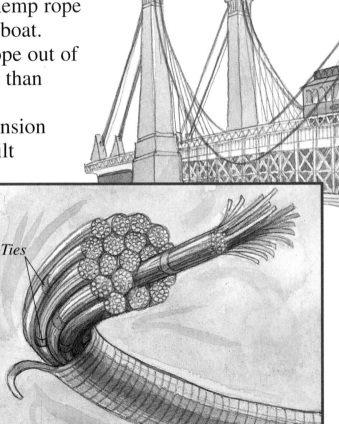

ROEBLING began making wire rope in a small factory in Saxonburg, Pennsylvania, in 1841. He moved his factory to Trenton, New Jersey, in 1849.

ROPE is made by twisting together small strands of fiber or metal. Roebling's bridge cables were made by tying together hundreds of small metal wires.

Handy Hint

Since you're only 32, some people think you are too young to take over for your father. If you grew a beard, you might look older.

So the roadway's down here...

...and the railroad's up there.

One day all bridges will be like this.

A Tragic End

Aaaargh!

JUNE 1869. Roebling's foot is crushed between a ferryboat and the dockside. His toes have to be amputated.

TO KEEP his mind clear while planning the bridge, he refuses medication to dull the pain.

HE BELIEVES he can cure himself with "water therapy"— constantly pouring clean water over the wound.

HE CONTINUES to advise on the bridge, but his foot becomes infected, and on July 22, he dies of tetanus.

7

Why Does Brooklyn Need a Bridge?

With almost 400,000 people, Brooklyn is the third-largest city in America. But many Brooklyn residents work in New York City, and every day thousands of people pay two cents each to ride one of the 13 ferryboats across the East River. So many people travel back and forth that the boats operate around the clock, making nearly a thousand crossings a day.

Some days the river is so foggy that the ferry operators can't see where they're going. Wind and rain make the trip unpleasant, and in the winter the boats often get stranded during snowstorms. If it's really cold, the East River can actually freeze over.

With the population of both cities growing rapidly, urgent improvements are needed.

THE EAST RIVER isn't really a river, but a tidal strait that connects the Long Island Sound to New York Harbor. The river bottom is very sandy, the current is swift, and the tides are strong. Many people doubt it is possible to build a bridge in the face of all these obstacles.

A Growing Population

THOUSANDS of immigrants arrive in New York every week—and many find their way to Brooklyn.

NEW YORK is the largest city in the United States. At least one third of its population is foreign-born.

CASTLE GARDEN is the city's immigration center from 1855 to 1890. (It will be replaced by Ellis Island in 1892.)

Why a Suspension Bridge?

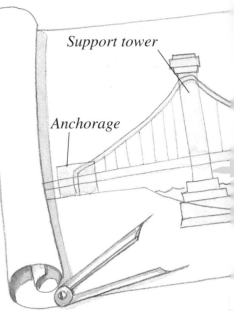

An ordinary low bridge can support very heavy loads, but it would block all shipping on the river—and in the deep water it would be nearly impossible to sink the dozens of pylons (supporting pillars) needed. A suspension bridge needs only two support towers. The bridge deck is suspended (hung) from cables that are attached to anchorages on each shore. A suspension bridge can span the deepest and swiftest waterways, while leaving plenty of room for ships to pass underneath. And because the weight is shared between hundreds of strong cables, the main span of the bridge can be very long.

Support tower

Anchorage

TO SUPPORT the weight of the bridge, the cables will be fastened at each end to anchorages— massive cast-iron plates that are held in place by many tons of limestone and granite.

OTHER OPTIONS. A swing bridge (above left) can swivel to allow ships of all sizes to pass through. A drawbridge, or bascule bridge (above right), can be raised when ships need to pass. But a tall suspension bridge is more convenient than either of these, because ships can pass right under it at any time.

THE EAST RIVER provides a deep natural harbor for the Brooklyn Navy Yard and the port of Brooklyn, which handles more ship traffic than New York.

11

Digging Underwater (1870-1872)

The bridge towers must rest on bedrock—solid rock that is part of Earth's crust—deep below the riverbed. But how can you dig underwater? The answer is a caisson—a huge waterproof box of wood and iron that is open at the bottom. The caisson is sunk to the riverbed, and then compressed air is pumped in, which forces the water out. Workmen enter and exit through airlocks. The digging is done by hand, using picks and shovels, and then steam-powered dredging machines scoop up the debris. A crew of 264 men work around the clock in three shifts. As they dig, the caisson gradually sinks into the riverbed, at a rate of about 6 inches (15 cm) a week. At the same time, workmen start building the base of the tower right on top of the caisson!

The caisson at the Brooklyn end of the bridge is 168 feet (51 m) long, 102 feet (31 m) wide, and weighs over 3,000 tons. The New York caisson is slightly larger.

Base of tower

They're working us into the ground.

I've got that sinking feeling.

Whale-oil lamps

THE CAISSONS are built at a nearby shipyard, then towed into position and sunk.

THE WORK is tedious and backbreaking. Even though the diggers are paid well ($2.00 a day), in some weeks at least 100 men quit.

Wow, it's hot in here!

The wooden walls of the caisson are 9 feet (2.75 m) thick. They are sealed with hot pitch and then covered with boiler plate (strong sheet iron).

Entrance

Airlock

Handy Hint

A jackhammer (which runs on compressed air) could speed up the digging. DrFFF!

Dredging shaft
Dredger scoop
Wooden sides

Bottom edge, plated with iron to help caisson sink into riverbed

Gasp!

AIR PRESSURE INCREASES as you dig down deeper under the water. This makes it harder for the workers to breathe. At the end of their shifts, the workmen are eager to return to the fresh air at the surface. Even after a pay raise, men continue to quit.

FIRE SAFETY. The men must be careful with their lamps and candles. In December 1870, a fire damages much of the Brooklyn caisson, which has to be flooded to extinguish the blaze.

Everybody out!

13

The Perils of Digging Deeper

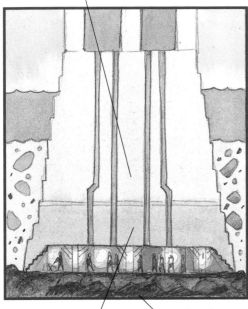

Base of tower

Roof of caisson   *Bedrock*

THE BROOKLYN CAISSON hits bedrock at 45 feet (14 m), but on the New York side, the bedrock is over 84 feet (26 m) down. Most of the severe cases of decompression sickness occur in the New York caisson.

Something is making the men sick. At the end of each shift, many laborers experience headaches, vomiting, dizziness, and severe joint pain. Doctors call this decompression sickness or caisson disease. Others call it "the bends," because the severe pain often makes men double over in agony.

The problem is the change in air pressure. Moving too quickly from the high pressure inside the caisson to the lower pressure on the surface causes tiny bubbles of nitrogen gas to form in the blood. It is these bubbles that are causing the painful symptoms. The project doctor thinks that the men should spend more time in the airlock when leaving the caisson, to allow the nitrogen to pass out of the body naturally. (He's right—but it will be years before doctors are certain about this.)

Aaargh!

AS MORE MEN SUFFER from caisson disease, the pace of work slows to a crawl. Some people are beginning to doubt that you can complete the bridge at all.

ABOUT ONE THIRD of the men who work in the caissons become seriously ill, and at least three men die from the disease.

I should n-n-never have taken this job!

Emily Roebling Saves the Day

Now you're stuck! You are the chief engineer of the bridge, responsible for overseeing the day-to-day problems of construction—but you are so sick that you are confined to bed at your house in Trenton. The bridge is already behind schedule, and if you can't supervise the work and communicate with your men, the project will be delayed even more.

But your amazing wife, Emily, knows what to do. She travels to New York regularly to relay your orders. Emily already has a solid understanding of engineering and math, and in her spare time, she reads engineering books to learn more about bridge construction. It's unheard-of for a woman to take charge of a major construction project, but Emily takes your place for three whole years.

EMILY TAKES OVER. She nurses you during your illness, even as she deals with the problems of construction. Without her, the bridge would never be finished.

SO MANY MEN suffer from caisson disease that you decide to stop digging in the New York caisson while it is still 6 feet (2 m) above the bedrock. It's still solid enough!

That's settled, then?

Yes, ma'am!

THE DIRECTORS want to replace you, but Emily convinces them to keep you on as chief engineer.

6 ft (2 m)

Bedrock

Tower Construction (1870-1876)

Each tower will weigh over 80,000 tons and stand 276 feet (84 m) above the river. The towers must be strong enough to support the weight of the cables and the roadway, and tall enough to provide clearance below for the tallest sailing ships. As many as 80 men work atop the towers, but conditions are dangerous. After two men fall to their deaths, you make a rule that no one can work on the towers if they get sick or feel dizzy.

Well, at least we can't get the bends up here!

THE TOWERS are built on top of the caissons. The first stones are laid while the top of the caisson is still above water. Once the workers in the caissons have finished digging, the caissons are filled with concrete to make them solid.

AS WORK PROCEEDS, huge watertight boxes called cofferdams are built around the base of each tower. The water is pumped out, and the space inside the box is filled with earth. Working inside the cofferdam (right) is just like working on dry land.

Why not hire sailors? They are used to working in ships' rigging, several hundred feet in the air.

Ahoy there!

JOHN ROEBLING designed the bridge for beauty as well as strength. The granite towers and pointed arches make it look like a Gothic cathedral.

WHEN COMPLETED, the towers will be the second-tallest structures in the area, only a few feet shorter than the spire of Trinity Church in New York.

The wonder of the age!

Holding the Bridge in Place (1873–1876)

Located 900 feet (274 m) inland on each side of the river, the two massive anchorages are designed in the same Gothic style as the towers. They provide a solid foundation for the suspension cables and are essential to the strength of the bridge. At the base of each anchorage are four massive cast-iron plates—one for each cable. The plates weigh 23 tons apiece and are held in place by 60,000 tons of limestone and granite. When completed, each anchorage measures 129 by 119 feet (39.3 by 36.3 m) at the base and is 89 feet (27.1 m) tall at its highest point.

Still, the work is late and costs are soaring. At least 15 men have died, and hundreds more are suffering from caisson disease. There are public complaints that safety isn't being taken seriously enough.

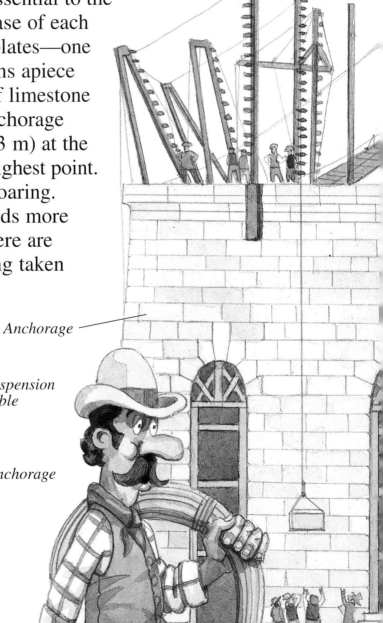

WITH THE TOWERS nearing completion, a temporary walkway is constructed to allow access between the towers and the anchorages.

Anchorage

Anchor plate   Anchor bars

Suspension cable

Anchorage

THE SUSPENSION CABLES will be attached to a series of anchor bars that run through the stone and connect to the anchor plates.

Walkway

Towers

You won't catch me going up there!

Handy Hint

Open the walkway to the public— it's good publicity.

Nearly there, Maud— don't look down!

THE WALKWAY is narrow and wobbly, but it becomes a tourist attraction, and thousands of people receive passes to cross this temporary bridge. It's a terrifying experience for some.

AFTER A THREE-YEAR ABSENCE, you are eager to return to the job site. You and Emily rent a house in Brooklyn Heights. Now you can see the bridge from your bedroom window.

Holding Up the Bridge (1876–1878)

Steel cables are the key to supporting the 1,595-foot (486-m) roadway that will extend between the towers. John Roebling's design called for four massive cables to support the weight of the bridge. Each cable is 15¾ inches (40 cm) in diameter and is made up of 19 strands. Each strand in turn is actually 278 separate steel wires—each ⅛ of an inch (⅓ of a centimeter) thick. The wires in each strand will not be twisted like rope fibers, but will be tied together every 15 inches (38 cm). It will take almost 15,000 miles (24,140 km) of wire to support the bridge—over 3,500 miles (5,630 km) in each cable.

To make a cable, the first step is to install a traveler—that's an endless loop of wire rope, 6,800 feet (2,073 m) long that works like a conveyor belt to transport cable wire from one anchorage to the other.

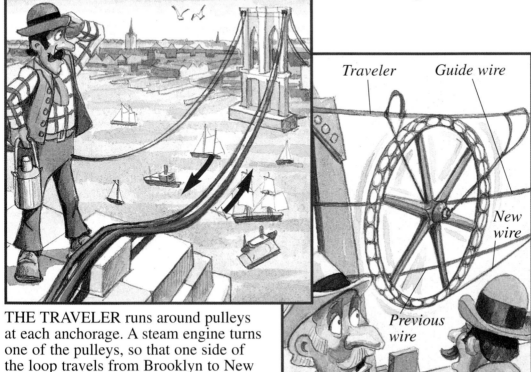

THE TRAVELER runs around pulleys at each anchorage. A steam engine turns one of the pulleys, so that one side of the loop travels from Brooklyn to New York, while the other side moves back the opposite way.

Traveler   *Guide wire*

New wire

Previous wire

A LARGE WHEEL hangs from the traveler. As the traveler moves between the two anchorages, so does the wheel. Each time the wheel crosses the river from Brooklyn to New York, it brings with it a loop of wire. A huge number of these wires will be bound together to make the suspension cables. Each individual wire is tiny. But once the wires are tied into strands and the strands are bound into cable, the four cables will easily support the roadway.

23

The Wire Rope Scandal (1878)

On two occasions in 1878, one of the steel wires snaps. The wire is defective! It's not your fault. Because you are the chief engineer of the bridge, the directors didn't think it would be ethical to buy the wire from your own wire-rope company. Instead, the contract went to J. Lloyd Haigh of South Brooklyn. Haigh's employees were supposed to submit wire samples for regular inspections. But to save money, they have been submitting the same good samples over and over, while providing substandard wire for the actual construction. To be safe, you decide to add 150 extra strands of good wire to each cable.

The crooked Mr. Haigh ends up in prison for fraud, but it's bad publicity for you and the bridge. The scandal raises the old questions about safety and gives the public more reason to doubt whether the bridge will be completed on time.

NO ONE KNOWS how much bad wire has gone into the making of the cables.

CONSTRUCTION is several years behind schedule and the cost of the bridge is still rising. If it's not finished soon, you may lose your job.

JUNE 1878. A suspender cable snaps. It recoils with such force that it kills two men instantly and seriously injures two others.

TWANG!

SNAP!

Handy Hint

The only way to ensure good-quality steel wire is to manufacture it yourself in your family's factory.

25

Suspending the Roadway (1878-1883)

Suspension cables

"Just hang on a bit, can you?"

Suspender cables

The last step is installing the roadway. First, steel floor beams are fastened to suspender cables that hang from the suspension cables. Then supporting frames called trusses are set on the beams and riveted in place. The roadway is then constructed over the trusses. To provide further support, 400 diagonal wires, called stays, are connected to several points along the roadway. These help to stiffen the whole structure.

The roadway is divided into five sections: two for road vehicles, two for trains, and an elevated walkway in the middle for pedestrians (see the small picture on page 29). Train stations are built at each end of the bridge. The trains will run continuously day and night, carrying up to a thousand passengers at a time.

THE SUSPENDER CABLES are fastened to iron bands wrapped around the suspension cables. To add strength, the diagonal stays are lashed to the suspender cables.

IT HAS TAKEN YEARS, but the project is finally beginning to look like a bridge. You can be proud that your father's dream is becoming a reality.

At last!

Diagonal stays

THE ROADWAY is built by four teams of workmen at once. On each side of the river, one team starts from the tower and works toward the anchorage onshore, while another team works from the tower toward the center of the bridge.

Suspension cables

Suspender cables

Trusses (resting on floor beams)

If it doesn't meet in the middle, they'll have our guts for garters!

Handy Hint

The Brooklyn Bridge is nearing completion. Now is the time to make plans for the opening-day celebration.

TWENTY-SEVEN MEN have died building the bridge. Most of the deaths were caused by falls from the towers, anchorages, or cables.

27

The Grand Opening! (1883)

After 14 years, the work is finished! The Brooklyn Bridge opens at 2:00 p.m. on Friday, May 24, 1883. Thousands of people line up to walk across the bridge as part of the opening ceremony. Led by President Chester Allen Arthur, himself a New Yorker, the procession slowly makes its way from New York City to Brooklyn.

Both cities declare a holiday, and 150,000 people pay a penny each to cross the bridge. Bands play, and thousands of onlookers watch from boats in the river.

In the evening there is an hour-long fireworks display—14 tons of explosives are set off from the center of the bridge and from the top of each tower. The celebration lasts till dawn the next day.

BANG!

THE FIRST PERSON to cross the bridge in a carriage is your wife, Emily.

28

WHIZZ!

Handy Hint

After all this work, you both need a vacation. Take some time to travel and rest up!

So long!

Then

Now

TODAY, 144,000 cars and trucks, 2,500 pedestrians, and 2,000 bike riders cross the Brooklyn Bridge each day—but no trains.

Glossary

Airlock An airtight chamber with two doors, through which people can move between an area with high air pressure and an area of lower pressure, without letting the high-pressure air escape.

Anchorages Heavy stone pillars used to anchor the ends of the cables of a suspension bridge.

Bedrock Solid rock that is part of Earth's crust.

Bends, the A nickname for decompression sickness.

Directors The top managers of a company.

Boatswain's (or **bosun's**) **chair** A plank hanging from ropes, used as a seat by a person working on the side of a ship or among the ropes above.

Boiler plate Strong iron or steel plating that is used to line the boilers of steam engines.

Cable A large, strong rope, especially one made of wire.

Caisson A waterproof chamber used by people working underwater.

Caisson disease A 19th-century term for decompression sickness.

Canal A human-made waterway.

Chief engineer The person in charge of a construction project.

Cofferdam A watertight box from which water is pumped out to provide a dry place for people to work.

Compressed air Air which has been put under more pressure than the air in the atmosphere.

Decompression sickness A painful and sometimes fatal disease affecting those who move too quickly from a high-pressure area to a low-pressure area. It is caused by nitrogen bubbles forming in the blood.

Drawbridge or **bascule bridge** A bridge that can be opened in the middle by raising a section of the roadway or deck.

Gothic A style of architecture that uses tall, slender towers and arches with pointed tops.

Granite A hard, heavy building stone.

Hemp A plant that produces heavy fibers that are used to make rope.

Jackhammer A drill powered by compressed air, used for digging or breaking up rocks.

Pitch A thick, sticky substance used to preserve and waterproof wood.

Pylon A post or tower that is set in a riverbed to hold up a bridge.

Roadway or **deck** The part of a bridge on which traffic runs.

Shaft A vertical tunnel.

Span A section of a bridge between two of its supports.

Stay A heavy rope or wire that helps to support a ship's mast, a bridge section, or a telephone pole.

Strait A narrow stretch of water joining two larger bodies of water.

Suspension bridge A bridge that is supported by strong cables running along its length (suspension cables) and by shorter, vertical cables (suspender cables) that hang down from the suspension cables.

Swing bridge A bridge that can be opened by swiveling a section in the middle.

Tetanus An extremely serious disease usually caused by an infected wound.

Traveler An endless loop of rope that can be moved along with pulleys.

Truss A framework of wooden or metal beams used to support a roof, bridge, or similar structure.

Whale oil Oil made from the blubber of whales; whale oil was used in lamps to provide light before the invention of the electric light bulb.

Index